The Loneliest Girl

Mary Burritt
Christiansen
Poetry Series

Mary Burritt Christiansen Poetry Series
Hilda Raz, Series Editor

The Mary Burritt Christiansen Poetry Series publishes two to four books a year that engage and give voice to the realities of living, working, and experiencing the West and the Border as places and as metaphors. The purpose of the series is to expand access to, and the audience for, quality poetry, both single volumes and anthologies, that can be used for general reading as well as in classrooms.

Also available in the Mary Burritt Christiansen Poetry Series:

Walking Uphill at Noon: Poems by Jon Kelly Yenser
origin story: poems by Gary Jackson
Nowhere: Poems by Katie Schmid
Ancestral Demon of a Grieving Bride: Poems by Sy Hoahwah
The Definition of Empty: Poems by Bill O'Neill
Feel Puma: Poems by Ray Gonzalez
Grief Land: Poems by Carrie Shipers
The Shadowgraph: Poems by James Cihlar
Crosscut: Poems by Sean Prentiss
The Music of Her Rivers: Poems by Renny Golden

For additional titles in the Mary Burritt Christiansen Poetry Series, please visit unmpress.com.

KATE GALE

the loneliest girl

poems

University of New Mexico Press | Albuquerque

ISBN 978-0-8263-6369-5 (paper)
ISBN 978-0-8263-6370-1 (electronic)

Library of Congress Control Number: 2021948235

Founded in 1889, the University of New Mexico sits on the traditional homelands of the Pueblo of Sandia. The original peoples of New Mexico—Pueblo, Navajo, and Apache—since time immemorial have deep connections to the land and have made significant contributions to the broader community statewide. We honor the land itself and those who remain stewards of this land throughout the generations and also acknowledge our committed relationship to Indigenous peoples. We gratefully recognize our history.

Cover illustration: *Medusa in England* by Nancy Farmer; gouache, 6 × 6 in., 2008
Designed by Felicia Cedillos
Composed in Utopia 10/14

contents

Part Three | Ever After

part one
Before

There are ten things you need to know to be a woman:

1. When you're young and the little boys say, "Let me see you pee," you need to say no. They want to see under your dress. Bad things can happen. They come for you.

2. When you're in school, and the other girls laugh at you because you're dressed like a half-wit, don't expect your momma to care. She'll laugh with her sisters, with her mother—they'll all laugh at you. They are laughing right now. They come for you.

3. When you grow breasts, and the boys say they just want to look at them, they don't mean it, they mean they want you to undress. They mean they want to have sex with you and then with someone else, and then with someone else, and then with someone else. They will tell everyone how easily you slipped off your blouse, unhooked your bra, stepped out of your skirt. You thought it was love. They thought you were easy pickings. They come for you.

4. In college at the parties, if you have a drink and then another, his penis will slip inside you, and if you have had too many drinks, so many penises will slip inside you it will be a party of penises inside you, a memory of penises, a throw down of penises, and you will try to stand afterward, you will try to walk. You will hear them laughing. They come for you.

5. You move to another state and start over; you date doctors and lawyers. You are taken to the country club where the fancy men put their hands on you. They take you to high-rise hotels where they grope you in exchange for dinner. You put out. You are popular. They come for you.

6. You get a job. You ask the women at your company to help you. You want help meeting important people, making connections. The women will not help you with anything. They sew the scarlet *A* to your blouse. They come for you.

7. You get married and then you get a divorce. You hope the women will invite you over to meet their single friends. They do not want you alone with their husbands. They don't trust you with their boyfriends. When you try to talk to their men, they come for you.

8. The only way you could avoid attention is to get fat, but you live in a city where fat is not permitted. For a few years, you let yourself get a little bit fat, and you have a few more friends. You have a fat boyfriend. Then you join a gym and lose weight. The women turn on you. They come for you.

9. You could become religious, talk to God. Become a Jesus lover or a God follower, and there in church, maybe the other women would like you, the other men would assume you aren't about sex. Don't people pretty much stop having sex once they join a church? You attend church one Sunday. Everyone can see you are a fake. They come for you.

10. You are a motherfucking, skinny-assed bitch. You've stomped around the world in your life, building castles. You've painted the sky and planted trees. You have broken the goddamn rules, and when they wrote new ones, you broke those. You are out of control; you are the wild new testament of women. You are breaking the eleventh commandment, which is thou shalt not speak if thou art a woman. You are speaking in your dirty boots without shame. Where is your shame, woman? Where is your shame? Why do you not hang your head, woman? They come for you. They come for you. They come for you.

Aristotle's Catfish

Aristotle's catfish is my song-fish
is my joy bite as I season and roll
the cornmeal, thyme. The crisp of
fin, of tail, I tongue deep, lick the bowl.
The bones I give to the cat,
who licks and crunches.
Who licks and crunches. Aristotle. Aristotle
is Aristotle's catfish. Even now. I song fish.

Shame

I entered her world.

I came chewing light, chewing bread,
chewing anything my lips could get around.

They said stop eating.
You'll be a fat girl.

My lips planted
around corncobs and chicken legs.

By age ten: pine sap, cat and dog food, hay, grass, dandelions,
clover, wild chives, tree bark, mold,

horse mash, forest mushrooms, leaves, sand, mica, fish eyes plucked
from newly caught fish.

I cooked a snake and ate it. I wanted
to eat earth.

They said, Don't. You'll be a fat girl, no one will like you.
Go light on waffles. In the woods, I ate everything. At the table, they
watched me.

Zippers exploded, buttons flew.
You must dress, they said. Only God can see you naked.

I could be watery thin, have a twig body, delicate branches for arms.
I could be a plucked flower, a vine. Why do you insist on being a tree?

We will live in our bodies.
We may not pay taxes.

We may not have children
We may not make music.

But we will live in our bodies. Of which,
from the beginning to the end of the Bible we must feel shame.

When I see a thin girl, I feel shame
for my splendored thighs and backside.

We live with our pulse,
our windowed eyes. Our heads and their place in the firmament.

Our bodies, lumpy heaps of globular energy,
a thicket of longing in which we wobble around Earth.

I scoop bread and eat. Take, eat: this is my body broken for you.
Aren't all our bodies god? Isn't every shape divine?

God declared early and late the body the seat of shame.

Aidos

For Greeks, *"aidos"* was a fear for oneself and one's place
in the world if one did not act rightly.
We have come to translate this word as "shame."

God watches you from heaven.
Sees the snail you squished, the fly you distributed across the wall.

I act wisely. Do not kick dogs or punish horses.
Open doors.

But God does not watch me. Not
when stones pile up. Not

when the first stone hits. Nor
when I am surrounded, dragged from the village. What is God doing?

Puffing air in the heavens
while I feel shame

for having brought the stones
to my door. I said the words. I gathered derision. Heaped

stones in piles. Invited the crowd. When
they began to jostle

to throw rocks over hand,
underhand, what could I say?

Except: God? Are you watching now?
Now? Now?

Medusa's Mother

I'm hemmed in by fire.
Someday I'll have husband and daughters.
After I give up

I'm still clotheslining,
bread-baking for my father.
I want to lead.

To emote fire, to change Greece.
We want everything men have. Not their bodies.
Power.

Men laugh. She can't even get a husband.
Poor thing. Nobody wants her.
There she goes, spitting out words.

Nobody wants the words of a woman.
They're chaff, scattered to the winds.
In a circle, men talk.

Money, boats, scaffolding.
Houses, roads, bridges.
Wheat, corn, silver, gold.

I join the circle, throw
out new subjects.
Healing and bread.

Gulls wheel overhead.

Men turn to each other
as if I haven't spoken.

Sometimes one will pick up my words,
repeat them, get a round of applause
for my words from his mouth.

The thrash of bed, of corn, of children,
the proper sphere for women,
not the public,

where her eye can rove,
where the machinations of her
devious brain can revel.

Women collect around barrels of rainwater.
Words spilling on our feet.
Our thoughts spin into bread and washing.

Finally I marry the man.
Hang out clothes to dry.
Watch ships leave the harbor.

Bear children of full-throated beauty.
Raise them and wonder
why the man devises wars for them to fight.

I long for a philosopher queen.
Don't miss the winning, the ruling.
I miss the thinking, the doing.

I wanted. Let there be light—
and the evening and the morning
were the first day.

The Other

We drink ice water.
Mother stares at me across the table.
Thirty-three years apart. Strangers.

When Minerva found Medusa raped in her temple by Neptune,
    she cursed Medusa, tearing away her beauty, turning her hair to
snakes.

Mother orders seared ahi, sends it to be cooked.
Married thirty years, leaf thin.
We pass story fragments.

    A woman without a story is no woman at all.
    Medusa, a terrible woman, feared but powerless.

What does the word "forgive" mean?
That it's all right?
That it didn't happen?

    Medusa in a different story after the rape.
    Virgin beauty to monster.

You leave. You are other.
Outside the great chain of being.
Other.

Mother tells me I left God.
That California will heave into the Pacific.

    We will be swimmers. We will have boats.
    My life is the building of a lifeboat, then a raft.
    From my sailboat, I can hardly see Mother on the shore.

What does the word "forgive" mean?
To give up desire or power to punish.
I have given up desire or power to punish my mother.

    I am Medusa. I could forgive away my snakes, but I don't.
    I'd rather carry the bristle of pain, the hair rain of hiss,
    than forgive myself. You fucker. Look what you've done.

To give up desire or power to punish.
To give up desire or power to punish.
To give up desire. Or Power. To Punish.

Darkness Thrown Down Like a Blanket

The cat found us in our sleeping bags.
Little girl beside me sucking her thumb.
I hummed to the cat and the girl.
Stars disappearing. Us on the porch corner.

We'd been sent out,
where the wind was.
She for laughing.
Me for making her laugh.

Then the wind.
Plunk of rain.
Always raining in New England.
Unbearable rain and green.

She said, We'll get wet.
We move back to the wall. She said,
We'll have to sleep all night
with our backs against the wall.

I said, We live our whole lives with our backs
against the wall.
She said, What if the stars come out?
I said, Even then.

Medusa Never Took Sexy Back

Medusa never took sexy back.
After the rape.
No sexy back.

People say, Get over it.
Over. It.
What you get over is it.

Penis. Thrust.
Ending of your song place.
Sweet place.

Darling.
If you could love me instead.
If you could love me in spite

of the throw of whip pain
against my navel,
the crush of bone against my back.

If you could not see this bristle of hair
I've grown to fight off attackers.
If you could not see me fighting nasty.

We could be lovers.
Like in old times.
Swing on the porch.

Nobody would be hurt.
Everybody fine.

A Wounded World

The rod of correction shall drive
the foolishness out of the child.

What did they use to beat you?
Stripped ferns if you were outside.

Inside, riding crops while you bathed, dressed, worked.
Crack, crack behind you stinging legs and shoulder blades.

Big sins required sawed-off broomstick or mop handle.
Six whacks as hard as a man could hit a child.

Always unconscious by the end.
Always in another place.

They brought you back.
To a wounded world.

Medusa in Love

My father used to say, Smile when you come into a room.
When I come into a room and see men, I smile.

The suitors line up for me. Boys and men.
Never a fan of beards. Hairy men are a no.

Mother says, Don't act like that, they'll call you a bitch.
Like what? I say. Like a bitch, she says.

At parties, I dance, the doors of the world opening.
Windows too. Whom will I marry?

My smiling works on everyone, but eventually I have to choose.
When you're young, pretty, smiling, there is everyone to choose from.

Ask Ovid, ask anyone.
I was raped in the temple of Athena.

What were you doing? Did you struggle?
Did you try to get away? What were you wearing?

Did you wear red? Did you wear heels? Was your clothing too tight?
Did you show neck, ankle, belly, wrist?

Poseidon held me against the white columns in his monstrous hands.
He raped me on the floor of the temple.

If you are raped in church, it's hard to go back to church,
talk to God. It's obvious God doesn't listen to you.

I heard children playing on the shore.
Sunlight poured through the white temple.

Everyone attended a party that night. My suitors were there.
Too bad, they said. They danced with other girls.

Don't ask me what happened next. Athena's curse.
The years huddled dark. My hair turned vile, a nest of vipers.

I grew hair everywhere. Women are not supposed to have hair
except on their heads, and that head hair should be contained.

The men who had wanted to bed me now competed to shoot me.
Pierce me with swords. Throw spears. Throw knives.

Killing Medusa cartoons were the rage. You could say anything about me.
Throw bottles. Break glass. I absorbed all human rage.

I had not only my own snake, but many snakes.
I had the power to kill men.

O Perseus, you rescued me from torment.
I will be born again. I will have a new name.

Under the Goblin Moon

Comedian raps Medusa:
Woman gets raped,
Woman turns into monster.
Monster woman is man hater.

Student writes paper on Medusa:
Raped woman becomes mad woman in attic.
Burned to death in Gothic novels.
Jumping off parapets to her death.

Novel spools out Medusa:
Woman raped in hot tub while boyfriend watches porn.
Woman becomes raging feminist, tries to change the world.
Wants children. Gets married. Does dishes.

Movie about Medusa:
Monster in cave; we don't know how it got there.
Many men come to fight. Epic battles.
Handsome prince wins. Kills monster. Marries virgin.

Medusa's story: I lived in a cave with other women.
I gave Perseus a creepy head to turn the Kraken into stone.
Do you know what my sisters and I do at night?
We dance ourselves divine under the goblin moon.

How Is It That the Rain?

For S

How is it that the rain . . .
How is it that the rain keeps falling?
With his hands around my throat . . .
How is that the rain?

How is it that the next day the sun . . .
Bruises on my throat.
How is that the sunshine through the leaves
bruises on my throat?

How is it that the trees?
How is it that the trees
hold sun in raindrops
like hidden jewels?

He says, Leave it behind.
Look ahead.
It happened.
It won't happen again.

Don't make me mad.
Don't make me jealous.
Just shut up. Can it.
    Then it's over. I'm gone.

He's telling the next woman
what a bitch I was. The next woman says,
You don't have to worry anymore.
I'll never stop, he says. I need to show her who's boss.

She wouldn't listen then.
She won't listen now.
She keeps smiling, doing whatever she wants.
I will stop her. She's still mine.

But you're divorced now, you're with me now,
the next woman says.
Shut up, he says, texting his first wife over and over.
You don't know who you're dealing with.

The New Ninth

"Killing Pluto was fun, but this is head and shoulders above everything else."
—MIKE BROWN AT CALTECH

Something big weird and tumbling
has crashed into the roof   we
see night sky
through tangled branches

though not many stars
it isn't going to rain you say
it is going to rain I say
we're both right   it will rain
then not rain
the roof will be open   all that sky
unbearably near   unfettered

a new planet outside Neptune detected by its ghostly pull
on other bodies   its orbit out of step with other orbits
this new planet is like Neptune but big cold dark
cave people prayed to the stars moon sun
I pray to the god of asteroids for breath
music water all that sustains story.

In All the Movies

Men push back the women, take the horses.
Women rake leaves, fill pails of water, stack wood.
Men ride off, row shallow boats, sail big ships.
Women crowd the marketplace, buy ribbons.

When the men come to a new town, they demand food.
Drinks, beds, music, stories. The women provide all this.
The men take their stories to the next town and sell them.
Sleep with new women. Eat their food.

Men thrust feet into boots. Walk all over God's world.
Women corral their children, teach them to read.
Women plant roses and summer squash.
Men buy roses for other women.

We cry along the riverbank. Give us roses.
Give us stories and books, make us sing.
The men ride by, laugh, pause to see us wet.
Stooping to wash linens and catch fish.

We wave them on. Don't stop and stare, we say.
Your rage is air. Give us something we can taste.
Give us darkness between your legs, they say.
We're all darkness, we say, We're nothing but darkness.

Speak Up, Honey

Mother: Speak up, honey. What are you saying?
That he showed you his penis?

Did he do anything to you?
Shove you down? Force you?

Was there something wrong with his penis?
Was there something wrong with you?

Do you hate men?
Are you a lesbian?

If it weren't for a man,
you wouldn't have this good job.

A man looks at your ass;
he takes out his penis,

he plays with his penis.
What you need is gratitude.

Close your mouth. Open your mouth.
Watch this man. If he goes far, you'll go far.

Hanging

After crime,
punishment.

I was hanged.
Survived the hanging.

My neck has rope-burn scars.
I will be hung again.

Kate should be punished.
I've heard since I was born.

As a kid, they'd say, You are going to be punished.
I'd say, Let's get it over with.

You fall.
Grace is where you fall from.

Earth is where you land.
Evil and fall the first story.

The only way out of fire is to fly.
The only way to fly is to grow wings.

Tall Poppy

She walks around with her head in the air
like she's somebody.

Who is she?
She came to town, built a library.

Who cares?
Who needs a library?

We have our own books.
We have our own parties.

She's never invited me to one of her parties.
Well, she invited me once.

Once I got there, she never talked to me.
Never offered me a glass of wine.

Her brain must be a crowded
little place, telling her, You're terrific!

She's fallen flat on her face now.
She'll be down for a while.

I used to think I could help her. I wanted
to say, Slow down. Do what I say. You'll be okay.

I wanted to say, Keep your head down.
In this town, they'll eat you alive.

But she kept laughing and marching around
like she knew everything.

Now that she's flat on her face,
I hope she learns her lesson.

I hope she learns to keep her mouth shut.
She thought she was the tall poppy around here.

People like her get their houses burned down.
They get stung by a buzz of bees.

Their heads are cut off.
Goodbye tall poppy.

part two

During

Golden Lion Has a Ball

We all were a golden lion once
Until the golden and the lion were stamped out
Before that we knew how to write, draw, dance
Afterward, we marched. In uniform.

Golden Lion learns to be quiet inside house
Goes to School
Shows off to other kids
Makes a mess of desk
Gets thrown out of classroom. Laughs
Copies in book, I will be a good Golden Lion a thousand times
Picks wild flowers in orchard
Does somersaults and jumping jacks
Has a ball.

Hear/Say

You say, Come here.
I hear, Get over here.

You say, You're pretty.
I hear, I want you naked.

You say, Let's meet later for a drink.
I hear, I want to fuck.

You say, Let me tell you about my . . .
I hear, Dick.

You say, I could tell we had an instant attraction.
I hear, I could tell you'd give in.

You say, I knew you wanted me.
I hear, I knew you'd do it with me.

You say, You take my breath away.
I hear, I'd like a blowjob.

You say, I'll call you.
I hear, Goodbye.

You Won't Amount to Much

A woman with no need for men
is a woman to be feared.

At the cult, the leaders talked to me
in the voice of God.

They said, You won't amount to much.
You'll never go to heaven.

You are the flat part of Earth.
God's hands cannot find you.

When I left, I searched for truth.
Who amounts to anything?

As it turns out, you won't amount to much if
    you're fat
    you're ugly

    you don't come from a good family
    you're fighting all the time

    you're differently abled
    you're different

    you don't play by the rules
    you think you make the rules

    you're squeamish about smiling at men
    you're squeamish about men

    you can't cook and serve
    you can't win and please

you aren't a pleasure model
you aren't a model of pleasure

you don't shut your mouth
you don't open your mouth

you had something bad happen to you
you can't shut up about it

Shut up. Lie down. There's a good girl.
All we ask for is your life.

Your body. Your silence.
Don't you want to go to heaven?

Don't you want to be one of those girls
we talk about and smile?

Golden Lion Ball

Golden lions sometimes have too much fun and are therefore suspect.
She looks like she's having a ball? Fuck her. Fuck her and the horse
she rode in on.

At the Golden Lion Ball, everyone has a ball
Plays games after sunset
Turns up the music
Starts to dance
Has a wild time
The moon comes up arcing across the grass
Golden Lions start to kiss
Keep kissing and dancing.

Sit on My Lap; I'll Show You Happily Ever After

Me: He likes me to sit on his lap.
    Mother: Sit on his lap.

I squirm around. He likes it. He likes to spank me.
    Let him spank you.

He likes it when I do cartwheels.
    Do cartwheels in your white dress with strawberries.

In the truck he puts his hand on my knee.
    He is giving you a ride to work? Shut up.

He puts his hand under my dress. I hate waitressing.
    Now that's bad.
    Be grateful you have a job.

I'm going to college.
    You think things are better in college?
    Just men with elbow patches doing it to you instead of men in
        coveralls.

The professor put his tongue in my mouth.
    Quit complaining.

The professor pulled up my skirt. He had me bending over the desk.
    It could be worse.

How could it be worse?
    He could be raping you.

How is he not raping me?
    Seriously? Are you asking me this? You leaned over the desk.

Were you raped?
    Honey, everyone's been raped. Everyone's been felt up.
    Everyone's had their ass pinched. Everyone's had some man do them
    when they weren't into it. Everyone's been fucked in their sleep.

I've met a guy, and he treats me nice.
    Sounds boring. But good for you if you're into that sort of thing.

He's a sweetheart.
    Make sure he isn't into porn. Most guys who seem nice are into porn.

He isn't into porn. He's into me.
    Sure.

We're getting married.
    Good for you.

He doesn't want sex anymore. He just watches porn.
    Blow your boss. Get a raise.

Are you crazy?
    Men help girls who're blowing them.

I got the raise. It wasn't too bad. It's just once a week. He doesn't smell.
    Does your husband smell?

A bit. Sometimes. He sweats.
    Does your husband know?

Of course not.
    Good then. That worked out great.

I'm going to be vice president.
    What did that cost you?

Anal.
    I've never had to go that far. In the old days it was all about blowjobs.

I'm taking care of my family.
    Good for you.

I'm still having sex with Paul. When he wants to.
    It would be silly not to.

When does it stop?
    Girls stay better looking longer now. It used to be thirty. Now it's fifty.

I'm nearly there.
    You're nearly where?

The safe zone. The hands-free zone.
    The happily-ever-after zone. You're going to live happily ever after.

Medusa's Cookbook

Thin layers of pastry
like grasshopper's wings
salt
almond paste
nutmeg
cloves—an unopened flower bud
cinnamon—a spiraled brown quill
honey
crushed nuts

Golden Lion Gets a Job

For the Golden Lion to fit in, one must learn
to cover up all signs of golden and of lion.

Golden Lion learns to wear a mask
A shoulder harness for jumping out of airplanes
A shield, sword, knife, lasso, towel, hat
Golden Lion never speaks without the mask
Golden Lion wears gloves to cover claws
Special shoes so as not to scuff the carpet
Finds few other Golden Lions at work
But how would one know with the mask?

Wound Care

Crossed to the other side of the street to avoid the wounded.
Gone to sleep to forget the wounded.

Watched the wounded on television.
Watched wounding on television.

Read fantastical stories of wounding.
Wrote fantastical stories of one's own wounding.

Hidden wounds up your sleeve, down your pants.
Through your body, under your socks, between your toes.

In the curve of arms and legs.
In the radius of the abdominal cavity.

Lasting wounds due to damage to underlying structures—
bone, muscle, tendon, arteries, nerves.

Cosmetic results not the primary consideration for wound repair.
Bites cause high rate of infection. Animal bites. Human bites.

We did not mean to wound others, but we did.
We wounded our friends. We wounded our lovers.

On my husband's back is a salt heart. I swim
every day in the ocean, ride behind him on the motorcycle,

the salt heart where my breasts press against his shirt.
His heart has a new valve.

One long, dark scar across his chest.
A wound of slicing deeply.

Forcing back the rib cage, taking out the heart,
replacing the valve in the heart chamber with titanium.

He ticks like a clock. When I say,
I have been wounded, I mean darkness.

Cherry blossoms open for fourteen days.
Petals drop. Leaves begin.

Be there for the first opening of white on pink.
Be there when the white on pink is blinding.

Be there when petals drop and green arrives.
Be there into the green and falling of leaves.

The bark sings to you. The leaves sing.
The cherry blossoms sing. Of wounding.

Of healing. Of white on pink. Of blossoms.
Feel petals blowing toward you. Feel morning come.

She Said, Leave Me Alone

She said, Leave me alone.
I'm reading.
I'm writing.
I'm thinking.

He said, What are you making for dinner?
What are we doing tomorrow?
What are we doing this weekend?
Have you walked the dog?

She said, I don't know about dinner.
I've been trying to figure out this math problem.
I'm doing calculus in my head.
Don't interrupt me.

He said, Where did you leave my glasses?
Where's the remote control?
Why are you still working on this? It's the end of the day.
Look I'm not trying to bother you.

She said, Don't come in here one more time.
I'm asking nicely leave me alone.
Even the kids know to leave me alone.
I can't have two thoughts when you keep interrupting.

He said, I'm your husband and I just want some time with you.
I just want to be nice to you.
I just want to have a conversation with you.
I just want to have a glass of wine with you.

She said, I'll be out in five minutes. Now are you happy?
You like swordfish and asparagus.
We can listen to "The Rite of Spring."
I've got cherry pie.

He said, I like it when you're smiling and happy.
I like it when we're together.
I like it when we're having a good time.
That's what I like.

Golden Lion Makes a Mistake

Once a golden lion makes a mistake,
the vultures arrive early for the feast.

Golden Lion starts doing a comedy show
Nobody laughs
Golden Lion is escorted off the premises
Hobbles off to a pub, drinks sake all afternoon
Golden Lion's mask is stuffed in the briefcase
Beer on whiskers, stain of beer on front
Golden Lion sleeps it off, gets another job
A new mask. Resolves to wear new mask always.

I'm Worried about Who Hates Me

Unless there's mind quiet
There's no writing
Just email and scribbling
Notes on the fridge
I'm worried about who hates me

And to-do lists: buy water glasses,
Cream, dog food, lipstick
Not the kind that says look at me
The kind that says
I'm worried about who hates me

Capers red onion
Pickles tuna grapefruit
I'm on a self-hating diet
I haven't been writing
I'm worried about who hates me

I should eat or sleep. I need a rest
Or a vacation that I don't deserve
Maybe just get a good night's sleep
Not to wake restless, to listen for noises
And to worry about who hates me

The not-writing consumes my days
I avoid the page while I run, work out,
Do the laundry, discover unpaid bills
Unopened mail I can't write now
I'm worried about who hates me

If I hadn't fucked up like that
I'd be writing right now
Not worried about who hates me.

Golden Lion Is Written Out of This Book

After the stoning is over, the fields are quiet.

Golden Lion is no longer part of this book.
There will be no more Golden Lion contributions to history.
That story now takes place offstage where all
Golden Lion stories should begin and end.
Once Golden Lion cried out, I am loved. I am loveable.
I can say whatever I want to. Golden Lion was wrong.
There are no tears. Only silence.
That story continues. Someplace else.

Terrible Stories

Don't tell me terrible things
my grandfather said when he got old.
Tell me nice things.

Don't tell me if you're
lonely, cold, or homeless.
Don't tell me if you're out of work

or without a boyfriend.
Don't tell me if you have a boyfriend
or if you have a boyfriend living with you.

I started a journal
to have someone to tell
when I went hungry.

When all the boys bought me Happy Hour.
That scrape with the police.
When my dog got run over.

The crow I rescued.
The guy with the knife.
All the terrible stories.

My grandfather watched birds.
Who am I when I shut out the dark?
The stories?

My children hold stories for years.
The cops, the parties, the breakups.
The breakdowns, the mad love.

They give me what they think I can hold.
We have baskets of stories.
Some writhe like snakes.

I put my stories
in my lover's basket.
Except this one terrible story

which I won't tell anyone.
It's the story that
made my grandfather shut the door.

I began to tell him.
He shut me down. If I were Scheherazade,
he would have cut off my head.

I'm all alone if there is no God,
and he's left me.
I'm afraid of dying alone.

I'm so afraid I've made a party,
then a mess of my life,
so someone's with me.

They're laughing, but they're with me.
Watching me create this topsy-turvy world
where change is the only constant.

I'm living in a party now; I'm not alone.
You should see me making up stories.
You should see me out here in the rain.

Blue Stockings

I wear blue stockings now
to remind me of blue.
Of not smiling for weeks.

I don't want to forget and, careless,
swing my hips.
I don't want to show my legs.

I don't want to come up for air.
There is no air.

Blue stockings,
there is no air. No air: I wear blue stockings now.

Consider the Lilies

Sit quietly while others eat.
Understand. This is not personal.

Walk the gutter.
Note sunlight on street. Not for you.

You were born without arms and legs.
You were born without face.

Without money in your pockets.
You have no pockets.

You were sowed on rocky ground.
Your parents had no land.

They are landless. Will never have land.
They are not an island. Or water.

They are not—you are not—of this earth.
Nothing on Earth conspires to sustain you.

Chalk it up to bad genes. And no lamp.
No meadow. Wood. Glade. Dappled sunlight.

Make the best of your red-checkered tablecloth.
Of your corn. Canned fish.

Crackers. Tomato soup. Onions. Garlic.
You have eggs. There will be more of you.

Pray without ceasing. Imagine writing.
Or painting. Imagine music. Or don't.

You don't have time. You don't have eyes.
Or ears. Your hands work furiously.

But produce nothing. You can't reach
the sill of the well.

Consider the lilies.

part three

Ever After

Aren't We All the Moon?

Aren't we going to wax
poetic about the wasp
that stung me, hiding
in the dishcloth this morning?

Aren't we going to hide
metaphors the way
wedding rings are
flat circles for time detectives?

Aren't we going to spend
our last conversation trying
to find some great last words
on the broken piano key?

Aren't we all the moon?

Revelations

Glory, honor, power unto God.
True and righteous his judgments.
He judged the great whore.
Her smoke rose up for ever and ever.

In righteousness he doth judge and make war.
Clothed in blood. His name the Word of God.
Out of his mouth a sharp sword to smite the nations.
He shall rule them with a rod of iron.
Gather yourselves together to the supper of the great God.
Eat the flesh of kings, of captains, of mighty men,
the flesh of horses, the flesh of all men.
Cast alive into a lake of fire burning with brimstone.

The remnant slain with the sword.
The fowls filled with their flesh.

Mine Eyes Have Seen the Glory

Mine eyes have seen the glory
Of the coming of the Lord.

Lemons in the middle of the table.
Thrash and blur of men fighting.

He is trampling out the vintage
Where the grapes of wrath are stored.

Men explain the universe,
Your place in it.

He has loosed the faithful lighting
Of his terrible swift sword.

Take the land. Take the company.
Fire the extras. Own the building.

Leave oil slick on the ocean.
Own the world.

His truth is marching on.

The Loneliest Girl

She never.

She eats apples with their cores.
Sent to the room.

Spits out seeds.
Apple eater, to your room.

Other kids throw rocks.
One birthday a box of dirt. Rocks. Sticks.

She thought a joke.
Hoped for a book at the bottom.

Mean girls laughed as she searched
through dirt for pages that were not there.

She pulled her own hair.
Just to feel.

Out the window the sun setting.
Days.

She never.

The Problem with Women Is Desire

I hide in the woods, wash in the stream,
collect shadows around me, dead leaves, find an upturned tree,
make a house on one side of it with branches.

At birdsong I bathe, comb my hair with my hands,
begin to feel holy again. Begin to feel whole.
They come for me.

She is unclean, they say.
She lured Poseidon into the temple.
She moved carnally among the ancient pillars.

She rubbed salt into her skin to smooth it, oil into her hair.
She wanted a man. What woman cries out?
I cry out when they chase me through the woods.

A trampling of horse hooves, a staining of blood
as they pull me up through the branches and sky onto a horse.
I am taken to the cave and cursed; the sun is shining.

The gods laugh—their night among whores, women who wanted it.
The problem with women is desire. The problem with women
is they do not know when to sit down. When to shut up.

I am thrown into silence.
I dream of beaches, lovers, waves, crowns of flowers.
I dream of petals, of lips.

In my cave at night, I see stars. The stars know evil.
As a girl, I sashayed around the house,
opening my fan, practicing my dance, drinking starfruit juice.

I drink starlight, make my home here by the sea,
live on fish, eggs, air, make music out of clapping.
I drink the sea and song. The cave is not my prison cell;

the cave is my wet home, my querencia.
In one story I gave Perseus a head, a story,
something to ride home with.

I'm swimming now in the stars,
watching the moon below me combing light
along the beaches. I'm watching you now.

The Spanish Call Us Medusas

Enter the world of stories
Live like animals

I can't imagine smelling human
No reason to slip into anything nice
No one to see me but my husband

He hasn't shaved for days
I don't care about bathing
I've stopped combing my hair

Don't call for me   Don't come for me
I'm in the deeper recesses of my cave
All wild woman   I can't imagine that bright world

Down here there are dark versions of us
You were a goat a faun a satyr
I was not a wood nymph or a goddess
I was a hill a river the peak of the mountain

That touched the sky
When you climbed to the top
You put your elbows in earth
That's how we ended up in this dark cave

Wet dark with story

Colossal

We walk on graves
Valley and sea uncurled

Church behind us smelling of incense and prayers
I pray for forgiveness and to live well

On the motorbike we thrill down hills
And up   Our gross impatience

Results in the overturned bike
Blood-stained pavement tells me

We rode   Climbed swam
Made big mistakes

The dark was a mistake
After the dark was the story

He Was the Only Man in the Room

The moon came up around the house of she-bears.
He was the only man in the room.

He didn't know who to talk to; the women were talking with each other.
He was the only man in the room.

The women weren't turning to him to ask what he wanted.
He was the only man in the room.

The women started undressing, changing their clothes, talking.
He was the only man in the room.

One woman was vomiting. Another said, Morning sickness will pass.
He was the only man in the room.

Several women made bread, told stories.
He was the only man in the room.

Two redheads cracked jokes about short men.
He was the only man in the room.

In the large tub, women took turns bathing.
He was the only man in the room.

One woman cleaned up blood, passed another a cloth.
He was the only man in the room.

Women were shouting to make themselves heard; everyone was talking.
He was the only man in the room.

One woman was shaving her legs, another her crotch. Some didn't shave.
He was the only man in the room.

One old woman was moaning on a cot; they took turns washing her face.
He was the only man in the room.

One woman entered with two ducks and a shotgun.
He was the only man in the room.

The women plucked the ducks and started roasting.
He was the only man in the room.

Another woman entered with pheasants and plums.
He was the only man in the room.

A third woman entered with eggs and long cucumbers.
He was the only man in the room.

Lemon and tea or wine. The old woman played the guitar.
He was the only man in the room.

A woman gave birth to a baby on the bed in the corner.
He was the only man in the room.

The baby was a girl.
He was the only man in the room.

It got to be night; the women paired off.
He was the only man in the room.

There was one extra woman, the one with a big laugh and a ripe, red
    tongue.
He was the only man in the room.

The butch midwife got two women.
He was the only man in the room.

This is a story of loneliness. Imagine a different story.
She was the only woman in the room.

That is a story of fear. A story of danger.
The only woman, in order to be safe, must leave the room.

Snakes in My Hair

I wish I weren't so fat.
Beauty would shield me.

I wish I made more money.
I'd have walls and greenery.

I want to be the center of someone's universe.
The cave is cold.

I want someone to lick me.
The walls are wet and slimy.

There is no burble in the wood.
I'm hungry but dare not eat.

All the men in the world are eating pizza, nachos, cheese sandwiches.
All the women in the world are eating celery, radishes, lettuce.

I want a man to make my heart wild.
Like windows in Japan, spring, pink-and-white petals of morning.

This morning.
I exited the cave.

Found a machete.
Severed the snakes.

Washed my body.
Anointed my head with oil.

Sure my cups run over.
Don't put your hands around my waist.

Don't even try.
Cup my breasts. I dare you.

I smell of sweetness.
I eat thickets of blackberries all afternoon.

Have you ever wished to be transformed?
This is that story.

You can walk out of the cave into the bright sunlight.
The curse is a story.

The flowering tree is a story.
The wings are a story.

Flight is a story.
Let there be light is a story.

Delayed Choice: Quantum Erasure

My father wanted for me milk.
He said to Mother, Stay with her.
Don't put on heels and work Wall Street.
Don't be a doctor or a physicist.

After the rape, Father couldn't see me.
Doctor said, She will never have children.
Not after this.
Not after this so young.

My father wanted for me milk.
My mother wanted for me god.
They took me to the milk place,
the god place, the yum place.

And stars they wanted for me,
stars burned out long ago.
Shooting stars throwing light streams,
dead rock falling through heat.

Mother made this move when I came in the room.
Like flies were buzzing, she brushed the air. Quantum erasure
means you might not yet ever exist in this universe.
You hang like a shadow here.

Then you appear in another story, in another universe.
In that world, I'm a comet. I take on the night sky.

Story of Light

In the aching wind between Tigris and Euphrates,
the first man kissed the first woman,
a kiss that began the thirst for thousands of kisses.

My first kiss wasn't tender. Not a kiss on the neck or the hand.
Not a kiss with a question. Not a long movie kiss
or a shy twilight kiss. Not a warm summer kiss or a cold winter kiss.

My first kiss was an angry hiss. Those kisses that devour your neck.
Kisses that don't need an answering kiss. Kisses so cruel.
Kisses that punish. Kisses that press lips into teeth. Kisses that own.

Just so was I kissed in the temple. Pushed against the floor.
Poseidon kissed me like you would kiss someone you hated.
Someone you wanted to kill. A kiss that says, I take this from you, die.

When it was over, there was a slap to my backside.
I rolled over, heaped on the floor, a slab, a thing.
They carried me out, head and hair thrown back,

my arms limp. Blood dripped onto marble floors.
My lips ached from those angry, bloody kisses.
The outdoors were so bright; I can't bear that light.

I dreamed of moonlight kisses. Sunrise kisses, midnight kisses.
Teatime kisses. In-the-bath kisses, over-the-counter kisses.
Sleepy kisses, wet kisses. Kisses to wake you. Kisses to want you.

In the Cave of Cisthene, I start slowly, kisses on my fingers.
I kiss the light on my shoulders, my palms, all along my arms.
I kiss light where it falls on my body. I kiss light.

My cave full of women.
We kiss into the night in pools of moonlight.
We bruise lips, touch thighs. No one bores us.

No one instructs us. No one bullies or beats us.
No one pushes us against the wall or the floor.
We are the story of light.

Becoming Sky

After I left the cult
The rain began

    How did you get away?
    How did you survive?

I hitchhiked
Jumped out of a moving truck

The trick is becoming anything other
than that flattened thing afraid

Becoming this girl with pears pomegranates
Fish swimming and the sea

This girl from underneath the scaffold
From dark   From nothing

When he said, Take, eat, this is my body
What he meant was, You are all you need

Outside my window is a curly willow tree
Its tendrils trace the sky

It came from a stick on the floor
Left over from an old bouquet

This tree combs the sky with her fingers
This tree is sky rain sunshine

Sky is all I ever hoped for
Sky is becoming

Joy is us singing backward
Into so much darkness

Joy is what we do who we are
We blow light across darkness

The Giant's Causeway

The Causeway is made up of forty thousand interlocking hexagonal pillars
formed by the eruption of a volcano.

The basalt pillars of the Giant's causeway
Are slippery
Are different heights

Are washed by sea
When I climb on one
I am over you

I look down on you
I struggle to top the tallest pillar
From there it is precarious

I might fall
You might catch me
You might struggle to mount your own pillar

We keep moving
Above below around
A lifetime of pillar climbing

I disappear from you
Between us a sigh of waves
A cloud of water

I reappear but so far away
I cannot hear you   But are you listening?
You ask   The answer is no

I should be listening or holding your hand
But sometimes the waves the light
the sea   The other people the pillars to climb

We are the volcano building pillars
We are the ocean washing them
We are the couple leaving hand in hand

Those Who Loved Medusa

You, Poseidon, came to me in the temple.
I laughed at suitors. Men in love.

You said I was a thing of beauty, a cup for love.
You smashed the cup. You poured the wine.

In Athena's temple, you raped me on the floor.
My eyes met Athena's. She found me guilty.

After the rape, I gathered myself in blood.
Athena whispered, I curse you.

    Athena said, You wore red. Your skirts rustled. You smiled.
    Your hair will rustle. Your face will be unforgettable.

    Your silky hair will be snakes.
    Your voice a hiss. You are creature.

Carry this story forward: Rape is the fault of the victim.
Carry this story forward: The female turns the key, opens the door.

You raped me in the temple.
I am that thing. Hold my head aloft.

Laugh for generations.
Don't stop laughing until Medusa

is synonymous with death. Turn me into that thing you fear.
Make me monster. Make me creature you fear in the dark.

You fear the thing in the dark. Wet, ripe, swollen.
Waiting for pleasure. That thing demanding.

Fear the woman with her own snakes.
Men kept visiting me in the cave on the island of Cisthene.

Men kept visiting the cave. It isn't true they all died.
Imagine the men who entered the cave, found love in the dark.

Imagine the men who braved the forest, found my lips.
Imagine the men who found my lips.

The Stoning Circle

If a damsel that is a virgin be betrothed unto an husband, and a man find her
in the city, and lie with her; then ye shall bring them both out unto the gate
of that city, and ye shall stone them with stones that they die; the damsel,
because she cried not, being in the city; and the man, because he hath
humbled his neighbor's wife: so thou shalt put away evil from among you."
—DEUTERONOMY 22:23-24

The Bible is full of stoning opportunities. If you want to be part of a culture of stoning, the Bible is a good place to start. The Bible not only condones stoning; God insists on it.

You grew up in a religious cult. The leader reads stories of stoning morning and night. You can be stoned for disobedience. You dream of being stoned.

The church leaders call for a circle of testimony, which is a circle of stoning. "Is there anything else?" the leader asks searching faces.

"Kathy was laughing about something George said. She copied him." You think about how everyone laughed.

"Anyone else?" Everyone remembers something you did. No one wants to be left out. The speaker in the stoning circle is thanked for their serving of stone. Throwing a stone means they are part of God's circle. They are in the will of God.

You are asked to sit in the middle of the circle. The words come thick and fast like hail. You are being nailed to the center of the circle.

When everyone has spoken, there is a beating, six strikes with a sawed-off mop handle. Adults hold you down. You try not to scream. You scream anyway.

You are put in isolation for three days. One meal a day. You are light-headed with hunger. Everything is very clear to you when you stare out of the window.

What is clear is that everyone will turn on you to be the one with their truth. You get to be the one with the gift of truth when you decide to throw the stone.

Ways to leave the stoning circle: Die. Walk away and be shunned and shamed. Become one of the stoners.

You walk away and are forever shunned by your mother, sister, everyone you have ever known. You walk away from stones into light and dark.

You leave with a dog on a bailing twine string, a harmonica.
A sleeping bag. Two dollars. A Bible.

You get a job cleaning houses. Your employer attempts to sexually assault you.
You save four hundred dollars for a car. You live in the car.

You get an education. You have a couple kids. You leave your marriage. Everything you own and the kids fits in your car.

You give your only life. You do not have another. You and your children live without. You work every waking moment. Your husband. Your dogs and chickens.

You begin to do soul work to understand. You carry around the weight of water with you everywhere. You put your hands in water. It is cold.

There are three ways out of the stoning circle: Death. Close shop. Stay with your people and be quiet, head down.

Death is not an option for you. Not while you could move to Mexico. If I die will they be happy? Should one die to make people you do not know happy?

You are at the bottom of the well. Your words marched off-key. You wish you could unmarch them. From the bottom of the well, you cannot see much sky.

You used to sing, "It is well with my soul." It is not well with your soul. Suffering cannot be measured. Suffering is suffering.

When you see stones being collected, you walk into water until you are in deep and swimming. There were so many stones in New Hampshire, they built walls.

The stones were so many they had to be collected every year before spring planting. The stones were many.

You begin to understand the bottom of the well. The bottom of the well is dark. You are down in the well a long time. You give your one life.

You cannot get it back. What's left of your life? You are going to find out, and when you do, you are going to keep that a secret.

Stumbling toward Grace

Are you thinking of killing yourself?
 I'm not sure. I don't think so.

Would you like to go on living?
 No one wants me to live.

No one?
 Okay, my husband and children want me to live.

No one else?
 Well, now that you mention it, I have eleven friends who want me to live.

Eleven's a good number.
So you want to stay alive for the eleven people?

And your husband? And how many children do you have?
 Technically two.

Why technically?
 I have two stepchildren who are adults. They may want me to live.

But your children and husband definitely do.
 Absolutely. No doubt. I'd swear on it.

 Of course, sometimes my husband is annoyed with me.
 But he still wants me to live.

Good to hear. He wouldn't want you to end your life?
 No, it would bum him out quite a bit.

 He'd cheer up after a few months of course.
 He'd be out dating, and he'd find someone easier to deal with.

Most women are easier to deal with at first.
　　But then we all turn out to be whiners.

Of course.
So, you are going to live?

　　Probably.
Things are bad now. But they might get better.

And in the meantime?
Two children, one husband who is only sometimes annoyed,

and eleven friends.
And you have a dog?

　　Yes, a dog. A great dog, Jasper.
　　I'd stay alive for the dog alone.

That is good to hear.
So, what happened? Can we talk about it?

　　We're supposed to listen and act wisely. I did neither.
　　And then a number of people wanted me dead.

I see.
But they didn't actually come after you to kill you?

　　No, they just wished me dead.
What you want is what matters.

　　I don't know what I want any more.
What did you do to annoy these people?

To make them wish me dead?
I wanted to be a defender.

Instead I was a heckler.
What would you like to do?

I have this one life to build the cathedral of the soul, to rebuild mine
like a small chapel, a single flower, a bell, a boat, a slip of paper with
one perfect poem, a singular line of prose, knees on the ground
planting a row of corn, a trembling ascent of a pyramid, a bird, a
grape, a perfectly poured cup of tea. I have my life to work on this
single thread. There is unrestrained stupidity and there is grace. In
my dreams, I stumble toward grace.

acknowledgments

Grateful acknowledgment is made to the following publications in which some of these poems previously appeared, sometimes in earlier forms:

2nd and Church: "Consider the Lilies"
Crab Orchard Review: "Terrible Stories"
Gibraltar Editions: "The Other"
Poetry International: "He Was the Only Man in the Room," "Medusa in Love," "Snakes in My Hair," and "Wound Care"
Rattle Magazine: "Sit On My Lap; I'll Show You Happily Ever After"

CPSIA information can be obtained
at www.ICGtesting.com
Printed in the USA
LVHW030446181221
706123LV00002B/10

9 780826 363695